Bread & Oil

Michael Rickicki

THY NAME
Publishing

Copyright © 2024
Michael Rickicki
Cover Design: Christopher Rickicki

Publisher: Thy Name, Inc. (McLean, VA)
Website: www.thy-name.com
Contact: info@thy-name.com

Rights and Permissions: All rights reserved. No portion of this book may be reproduced, stored in a retrieval system, or transmitted in any form or by any means — electronic, mechanical, photocopy, recording, scanning, or other — except for brief cited quotations in critical reviews or articles, without prior written permission of the publisher.

ISBN: 978-1-7368128-5-3
        978-1-7368128-6-0

Printed in USA

__Dedication__

This book is dedicated to my mother, for teaching me to look up at the stars and be unafraid.

Introduction

My testimony is the same story that you've heard many times and could be summed up in the simple phrase, "I was lost but now I am found." By the autumn of 2019, I was a seasoned drunk on a downward spiral. I was studying philosophy at university and had spent the last three years disproving all of the Christian values of my youth. I could have written a series on the things I did wrong. For now I'll say that I've made many apologies and amends and I still have more to make.

Oddly enough, during that same time I began to feel a call towards religious life. I had shut it out of my mind many times due to my own doubting and reckless behavior. However, come my senior year, I decided to take the call seriously. Being at a Franciscan university, there was a small community of friars, who are still active to this day. They live on a quiet hillside, only five minutes from my parent's house, which operates as a retreat center for the college community. It was there that the questions I had battled for so long would finally be answered.

I had no business being among these men. They didn't seem to care about that. They saw that I was looking for a connection to faith that was far deeper than what I had ever experienced, and welcomed me in. The brothers did not push any agenda, or speak to me of conversion. Rather, they gave me the space and the time to walk and eat among them for however long

I needed. During that time I cleaned up, let go, and moved forward.

It was with these friars that I learned the process of Lectio Divina. In traditional practice, Lectio is reading, meditating, and praying over Scripture. The brothers practiced this regularly, but they took it a step further. They would practice Lectio, not only with the written word, but with the living word all around us. They engaged with the whole of creation to witness God revealing himself through all things.

God is not a squirrel. However, He can reveal Himself through a squirrel or any created thing, from the smallest blade of grass, to the entirety of the universe. If Christ is in all things, then He can be revealed through all things. The brothers taught me how to sit still and pay attention to these movements. As a result, I left their home months later, refreshed and renewed, with a much deeper connection to God, people, and the whole of creation that has blessed me each day since with an overwhelming amount of peace. As Paul might say: they planted and watered, and God did the work.

This is a collection of various reflections I've had through engaging with the written Word and the whole of creation. My hope is that through my personal practice of Lectio Divina, you too will engage in this process. This is not a book on "how to do it," or a "here's what I learned from living with friars" book. I am not a friar, nor do I speak for or represent them.

Rather, this book is meant to give you the space to engage with things that, possibly, you've overlooked.

The poems are provided with space in this book for you to engage with these reflections as well. The space is an invitation for you to contribute whatever it is that's on your heart–from words, to drawings, or any medium you choose to express yourself. We do not live for a God that calls us out, but One who calls us in, to take a seat at the table. I'm inviting you to join me at my table, for a brief moment, and have a discussion.

I am a cook by trade, and half Italian by birth. After collaborating with my publishers, Amy and Maggie, it seemed like a fun idea to organize this book like an Italian dinner. Once again, inviting you to the table, to enjoy the bread of life with us. I hope that you will sit down, take the time to consider, contemplate, and contribute to the meal.

Peace and all Good,
Mike

Aperitivo

If you listen closely

All your life

You may hear His voice

And the voices of all the others

Antipasto

Blue Heron
Oak Leaves
Co-labor
Simple Meals
Bird Bath
Sisters and Brothers
Tending to
Sage bush
Merrily, Merrily
Breathing and Smiling

__Blue Heron__

The great heron sits on a rock
In the middle of the river
Observing fish beneath the surface
Encouraging us to find our own perch
Along streams of living water
So we may be still
And know.

<u>Oak Leaves</u>

I wish for a simple love
To awaken each day without doubt
Say yes
And do as I should
With the grace of oak leaves
Absorbing the sun
For as long as they are needed

<u>Co-labor</u>

I take not lessons
From leaders of the worldly
I watch bees and flowers
Working together
And pray
For such perfect peace

<u>Simple Meals</u>

The kingdom of God
The living gospel in everyday lives
Is within the man struggling to get by
Bringing a simple meal
To the single mother

Bird Bath

I bathe in the sun
By the pond with little St. Francis
Precisely where we should be
Still
Moment after moment
In the garden of your glory

Sisters and Brothers

I join with all of creation
In the song and praise of Christ
Who lives and awakens all of us
Sisters and brothers
From our neighbors to the blue jays
Every atom
Of the entire universe

Tending To

A smile from a great friend
A bear fishing alongside me
A hug from a mother
Or a pigeon watching me garden
Are all I need
To know your joy
And sense your peace

Sage Bush

Do you hear the call
From the throws of the ocean wind
Demanding your attention
To pause
And listen for awhile

Merrily, Merrily

The trout waits patiently
Just below waters rim for landing flies
So I wait
On the edge of this field
For the passing of little moments
Of grace

__Breathing and Smiling__

The gospel speaks
Living among us now
In every creature of the earth
Stars seen and unseen
Weeping of love
Poured out for all of us

Primo

Rhythm's
Merton's Heart
Fresh Honey
La Pos
Storm Clouds
Friars Pond
A Mother's Hand
To Do So
Kerry
The Chapel
West Notch
Old Man Mountain
Bearing The Burden
Footsteps
As I've Always Been
Simple Things
Andrew's Hill
Big Thompson
18th Sunday
Kevin's Homily

<u>Rhythm's</u>

The breathing of the earth
Of the entirety of the universe
The living word
Moving gracefully through
Infinite actualization

The rhythm of God
A song so quiet
And so omnipotent
Echoes off of all things
Living among us
Calling us in

Like a raft on a steady stream
The moments of past
Present and future
Move beyond our gaze with no chance
Of returning to or knowing that
We will make it forward

All we have is
What is here and now
Yet what is here
Is the entire creation
Breathing with us
Opening its elongated arms to us
Inviting us in
To experience it fully
Perfectly
As we are

Merton's Heart

There is an opening
Overwatching the river valley
Once great mountains
Now rolling hills

Creation begs
With open arms
To journey home

I hear the call
In bees drenching themselves
With midsummer flowers
Or children splashing
Within a glacial creek
And birds stealing
Bugs flying over the heads of trout

The great I am
Being
As we ought to be
In our daily lives
Like deer headed to water
Merely for thirst

So we journey
Through rolling hills
Across the Genesee Valley
To surrender at
Merton's Heart
As all life must
To the greatest journey
All life will ever know

Fresh Honey

The living word
Like a bear
Trudging in the brush
On the scent of fresh honey
Or whitetail sneaking
Through the shadows of dawn

Like scattered brushes of fall
Colors painting expansive valleys
Or snow-capped mountains
In the July sunset

Like bullfrogs calling
From a still pond below
Or crickets singing
Under the great mirage of stars
As if they were stage lights for a choir

Asking us
To consider for a moment
To pause and breathe
And feel its presence
In an ever-changing world
Yet a world
All the same
As it's ever been

La Pos

Standing outside of La Pos
With sunflower seeds in my palm
Offering food for passing chickadee's
Who rest their gentle knuckles around
My fingers and
Pause
For a moment

Looking out to the world with me
And waiting for friends who will
Partake in the offering as well
I smile upon them and they tilt
Their heads at me
Take a seed
And fly into the trees

The garden is here among us
Now
The kingdom has come and thy
Will is being done
Day by day
In little moments
Seen and unseen
Calling us in to rest in the glory
and to co-labor with the totality of
Christ

One Body
One Spirit
In a myriad of images

Storm Clouds

Storm clouds overhead
Covering the light of the sun
Forcing the small animals
To find shelter in piles of brush

Beneath the evening sky
Dispersing crowds from the banks
So I may stand
Alone on the river
Crazy for trout to the outsider
But to the observant one
I remain still on the water
Keen on the fly bouncing along the surface
Hunting for God
As Elijah
In the midst of the storm

Friars Pond

Alone by the water
But never lonely

Adjacent to brushing pines
In an autumn breeze
Weaving quietly through the needles
As bass swim effortlessly through weeds

Where it comes from
And where it goes
We do not know
An offering
Like myrrh to the king
From one
To another

Deep breaths of cool air
Seated across from the little poor man
Anointed in birds
Hoping to be worthy
Of such great lecturing

A Mother's Hand

Looking up
From the front yard of a modest home
As likely many before
Gazed upward too

Glaring lights of endless possibility
Terrifying in expanse
Commanding humility
From my anxious ego

The seen yet unknown
Malevolent and beautiful
Staring down upon us
Yet unbothered

"Isn't it incredible?"
She asks
"Yes," I reply
Unafraid
In the comfort of a blessed mother

To Do So

We could spend our lives
Groaning o're the direction
We must take for life well lived

Not I
Nor you
Should waste such precious time

We should stand on high peaks
For the sake of effort
Ride horseback through fields
Solely to feel the wind
To pull large trout from small streams
And hunt old whitetail in ancient forests

We should aim to love deeply all we encounter
To be direct in the bearing of fruit
To plant seeds our great grandchildren shall grow
To set our intentions on the highest good
No matter the sacrifice needed to do so

God does not ask us to remain idle
But to live
As not to squander such incredible gifts

Kerry

Over fields of green
I've never seen before
Kissing the clear sky
Along minor mountain peaks

I watch sheep graze
From one patch to the next
Free from concern

And the shepherd
Standing upon high ground
Watching over his flock
Still and stoic

I ask of myself
What role do I play
In such a great orchestra
Of musicians better than me

But He calls to me
Always in times of my own stillness
Saying to be here, now
Exactly where you are
As you are
And this is enough

The Chapel

From around the world
We make our way
Following a voice
Gentle and barely heard

Though we have no map
Or compass to guide
We see the path
Ever before us
To your humble home

Standing meek
On the edge of the hill
Overlooking dense forests
Extending your hand
Whispering softly to all

Be still
And know

West Notch

I take shelter in you
Like a sparrow in the bush
When I become too clouded
By the fog of my own world

Let go
Over again
And again

To find rest
Much needed each day
In your benevolent embrace

Hardly shall I know
A comfort so great
With only positive consequence

As the calf runs
For its mother
So shall I run
For your eternal love

Old Man Mountain

I sing your praise
When my eyes open each day
And I draw the first breath
Of a new morning

Oh how so many
Know not the miracle
Of arising here today
In this moment
Or any moment hereafter

I will marvel each rising of the sun
As if the last I'll ever know

My eyes lay upon you
In the presence of all
My peace I give them
Your peace with us always

May I not prove unworthy
Of such marvelous gifts

Bearing the Burden

Does the bird wish
To be a better bird today
Than yesterday

Or the elk to be
The most like an elk
That an elk can be

Or the pike
To be the fastest pike
In all of the water

What a condition of man

We endure the great burden
Placed on ourselves
To prove our worth
To a creator that already sees us as worthy

He asks us to experience
All the woes and gift of our true condition
To experience it
Wholly good
And righteous
As we are

Footsteps

Many have walked
The river where I now stand
Hopes and dreams
Fears and desires
All their own
All so the same

I feel the footsteps
Of those who stood here
Searching for more
Looking for you
Hoping for peace

I hear their words
Of different languages
Yet saying the same
As I am now

Unique in our own ways
Sure
Different however
We are not
Their hands in mine
As mine in yours
Gazing
Considering
Contemplating

<u>As I've Always Been</u>

I lay down in the evening
On land you have made
And find peace within your embrace

Though I know not
What tomorrow will bring
For myself or anyone
Or if tomorrow will come

Or if my ambitions
And desires
Will ever be made true

Or if I'm doing right
And bearing fruit
Walking the narrow path

I know for certain
That in this moment
I am totally in your love
As I've always been
By grace alone

Simple Things

In the early morning
Along a great river
The fog settles thick above the water
Pronghorn graze slowly
Up the surrounding hillsides

The smell of coffee
From outside our shelter
Friends too
Taking in the early air

People from all around
And all walks of life
Gather here along the banks
With friends and family

All of us here
Eating something small
Before wading out into the water
Breaking bread with one another

He is recognized here
In the simple things
Where two or ten thousand are gathered
His presence always with us

<u>Andrew's Hill</u>

I run frantically
In all directions
Without aim

Overwhelming
Is the fog of the world
At times

Yet you center me
You give me rest
In fields of tall grass
Under blue skies
Like a fawn
Nestled under its mother

You set me on a clear path
With an easy heart
You have overcome
That we too may overcome
With courageous hearts

Running the good race
Fighting the good fight
By our side
Always and forever

Big Thompson

I look up from the river
To steep cliffs
That have stood firm
In this great canyon

Above me are sheep climbing
Up the straight walls
To find safety and solitude

Their hooves rest on little holds
Reaching out subtly
From the seemingly barren face
Confident in the rock
And their strength

Do I bear such confidence
In the one who promises
The whole of the universe
And eternity
To all He has created

The confidence of John and Paul
And many others
Who showed us it's not just to be kind
But to give your life
To the giver of all

Do I bear such confidence
In a power much greater
Than hooves and stone

18th Sunday

I long
To be made anew
With each rising of the sun

Earthworms and insects
Doves and red squirrels
New flowers and fruits
All rise
To bask in your glory

Should this be
My last day on your earth
Would I not bask
In your morning too

With each breath
You draw me closer
Telling me
Away with the old
Be renewed in your spirit
Eat of the bread of life
And never hunger again

Kevin's Homily

All things
Belong in the arms
Of Christ crucified

The whole universe
From the largest star
To the smallest atom

The highest mountain
To the smallest flower

The greatest of men
To the least of us

All belong

And within us all
Is the totality of Christ
From the largest star
To the smallest atom

All matter
Matters

Asking of all things
To be anew
In the great promise
Of Jesus
The risen Christ

Secondo

Grandpa's Garden
Commands
Southern Colorado
Hurried Tracks
Among The Living
The Way to Eat
Joy
Streams of Fire
The Good Hunter
Emerson's Eye
Inauguration 2021
The Beggar
Streams of Awareness
Commencement
Perfect Ways
Consonance
Leisure
Lyell Ave
Mallards Over The Hill
Indian Hill
Craftsmen
Wyoming
Maplewood
To Make Beautiful
Trials

Grandpa's Garden

The good shepherd
Is like my grandfather in his garden
Who waits until the last frost has passed
To till the soil and plant seeds among the mounds
He waters the land and keeps an eye on the weeds
And he pulls them from the ground
to give room for his plants
When the time is right
He plucks away all the fruitless vines
And ties off the good ones until they have the strength
To support themselves
He fences off the squared beds
To keep intruders from destroying his labor
He walks the rows and tends to each of their needs
Some would harvest at the first sight of fruit
But he knows to be patient until each plant is perfectly ripe
He harvests appropriately whenever the plants are ready
And divides his bounty between what he needs and what he'll share
Family and friends gather at his doorstep each summer
To receive the fruits of his tender labor
Generously he gives
Gently he smiles
And humbly he rests

Commands

I walk quietly
Through a grove of small pines
Adjacent to the west face
Of a wintered hill
Watching my prey slip between bare trees
Hoping to go unnoticed

Go into the wilderness
And fetch us some wild game
Commanded thousands of years ago
And who am I
To question such

I step slowly upon the softened ground
Eyes keen on the gaze
Of the beautiful doe
Unaware that I am plotting
Such awful schemes against her

Commanded by friends
To take life
For the sake of a garden
We love
And we kill
And I have no answers
To such a condition

Southern Colorado

We lay down
In the womb of three great mountains
Rising to meet
The evening sky

Resting in
The calming embrace
Of stillness and silence

You my friend
Are as much the image of Christ
As the mountains

And I
As much Christ
As you

All of us together
At a single moment
In the expanding space
Of the present

All in one
And one in all

Hurried Tracks

As the sun sets
Over the great hills
Of my homeward river valley

The stream ripples
Reflect the light
Of this night's moon

I shall sing your praises

For you alone
Would design such awesome beauty
That should stop
The most ambitious of men
In their hurried tracks

That they too
May ask of themselves
How great and illustrious
Is my God

Among the Living

I stand in your garden
In awe and wonder
Like a child
Seeing the clouds from above
For the first time

A miracle indeed
To stand among the living
In this moment
Living as well

What great feats for man
To be challenged to overcome
For you and I to walk
Where we walk
And rest
Where we rest

What great feats for the son of man
To be challenged to overcome
For you and I to drink
Of the Lamb
To eat
The Bread of Life

The Way to Eat

The unknowing cub
Rises from its den to stand
As it's mother stands
And to walk
As its mother walks

The cub meets many things
It's never known
Afraid at every turn
Yet the mother shows the cub
The way to look
The way to climb
The way to smell
The way to stop
The way to fight
The way to eat
The way to rest

I walk the earth
And look to you
To show me where I must go
What I must do
Wholly reliant on your infinite knowledge
To light the way
That I may not fail

Joy

Upon a rock
At the edge of an alpine lake
In the midday sun
I sit and wait for the breath

A large osprey scrutinizes
The clear water for
A break in focus
From a Yellowstone cutthroat

The wind at such elevation
Rips quickly through the remaining trees
And breaks against
The surrounding statues of ancient rock

Patiently I wait
With no expectation
Or prior influence
Wholly in a single place
And wholly in the entirety of the cosmos

Moment
       Moment
              Moment

But never dwelled on
Merely the expression of joy
Being of all bodies
And one body
At once

Streams of Fire

People will devote their lives
To the service of someone
Some idea or concept
That is as mortal as they are

What sorrow of being to service that
Which will wash away by the current of time
But not us
Sisters and brothers

We are not caught in the tide
Of party or representative
Rather we serve the breath
That moves through all things
Since the time before time
And will remain long after our bloodline
Like the tree planter
That will never rest under its shade

The Good Hunter

The good hunter
Sits still within the shadows
Observing every flicker of light
That passes through the grove of trees

He waits with admirable patience
For the precise moment to draw his bow
Longing to meet with his quarry
After a lifetime of preparation
Success and failure

Such as him
I sit in a quiet corner of the pines
Watching every thought
Remaining keen on every moment

With great patience I long for the second
That time dissipates into eternal present
Where I lock eyes with the savior of life
And the only response
Is to smile and weep

<u>Emerson's Eye</u>

I'm sitting on a train
From Yonkers to Manhattan
Watching homes and businesses
Pass by in an instant

I look down the rows of chairs
As many eyes look back at mine
In their faces I see you
And in your face
I see myself
Joyful to know
That we are alive
Righteous
And well

Inauguration 2021

There is a man on a milk crate
With a microphone and speaker
And a rigid finger pointing outward

You are wrong
He cries
For all you have done
With such arrogant authority
He hammers against the brimstone

Calling out
You and me
On this and that
As has pushed away
So many before

The Christ I know
Sits like a happy Friar
In a circle of students
Asking the quiet one
To share her thoughts
Not to call her out for her reluctance
But to call her in
So she may let go
All that has burdened her
For so long

The Beggar

There is a dog
That sits by my feet
Under the table

Eagerly he waits
For even the smallest crumb
To slip from my plate
To the floor

As am I Lord
Hungry and begging at your feet
Waiting in excitement
For even a glimpse of your grace
To fall upon my head

Streams of Awareness

Streams of flowing awareness
Flow from your throne
Providing water
Of which we'll never thirst

In moments of quiet
Calming our bodies
These wonderful moments

We bathe in the streams
Of life everlasting
And call to the others
Let go and be still
Drink of the living water
That flows infinitely

Commencement

We are invited
To take our seats at the table
To join hands
With our sisters and brothers
And partake of the feast
Of joy, peace, and love

All of us
All things gathered
Within the arms of Christ
To be made new
Daily in our hearts and minds

What joy and power
To know we are one
Perfectly as we are
And to not just hold this as a sentiment
But to live it out
Noticing each other
And taking the time

Perfect Ways

I envy the flowers
Who every year grow
And blossom and stand upright
Perfectly each time
Then whither and die exactly as they should
And the sun who each day rises
Right when it should
And sets
Exactly when it should
And the moon who controls
The tides each day and night
Who provides the exact amount of light it should
Without questioning it

How I long to serve you
In such perfect ways
To follow without question
Or without being told to do so
To walk in perfect maturity
As one alive in Christ should
To do exactly as I am supposed to
As is the function you've set upon me

Consonance

The walk of this life
Is the consistent act of letting go
Like St. Francis and Clare
Who stripped themselves
Of worldly nobility and possession
To be made new and noble
In the eyes of the Lord

Each day I rise
With the same consonance

Subtract
Subtract
Subtract

Until all that is left
Is the being of being
Wholly perfect
One day I hope
Reflecting only the image
Of the One who created
And continues to create

<u>Leisure</u>

Walking in silence
At my own pace
Under the stars
Up the snowy mountain

Following my brothers
And some
Following me
Each at their own leisure

Searching in our hearts
Not for each other
But for the One
Who gave us life
And calls us in
To the reality of our being
The true nature
Of nature itself

We climb forward
Not with fear or doubt
Or ambition
But with great groans
Of longing

Lyell Ave

I weep for the extension of peace
My suffering does not come from persecution
But from the daily observation
Of dead people with their eyes open
From the highest of ranks in the nations
To the addicts clawing at the concrete

Where are you?
I wonder at times

The breath moves from one direction
To the next
And I know not where it is going
Or why it hasn't awoken
Every person
Who at their lowest
Still bears the face of Christ

The harvest is many
This I know is true

Mallards Over the Hills

The Spirit in our lives
Like a blanket being pulled over us
In the midst of a cold winter night
And floating away
Like loose feathers from a cardinals nest

Refreshing and frightening
Pulling us from the experience
Of ourselves as we think we know
Into the reality of who we are

Unbound by time and unlimited by space
Souls flying over the hills
Like mallards against the purple sunrise
Journeying to pastures unknown
Yet familiar as is a place recalled

Sit still and wait
Be here in this moment
Patiently awaiting its coming
Like eagles perched on a tree branch
Looking towards the water below
Waiting for a fish to rise

Indian Head

I sit at cliff's edge
Overlooking a clear blue lake
Nestled at the base of a heavy forest
Atop Indian Head
With cool morning air
Still wet from dew
Soothing me after a steep climb
Grace and peace be with you always
I join in fellowship with the living Christ
Who in all things sits with me now
And with everyone
Silently over the whole of creation
Like fog balancing along the tree limbs
Calling us to sit beside them for a time
Breathe deeply and smile
Be still
Be

Craftsmen

I watch the craftsman
Who with such focus
Decides where to cut
What to save
Where to fold
And what to throw away

So I wish
To know the Spirit of God
Where it goes
Where it comes from
Why some are saved
And some are thrown away

How some laugh so loud
And others so little
What is joy
And does it matter
Or peace of mind
For the shameful sinner

The more I learn
The less I know
Thus I choose to sit
Wherever seems quiet enough for me
And wait for it's arrival
So I may wonder
For a small moment
And offer it elsewhere
To whomever is ready to receive

Wyoming

Pause here
On rocky road
Through red dirt desert

Oh orange blossom
Erupting from beneath the horizon
Slashing with streaks of purple and black

Oh jaw dropping glory
Commanding stillness
From all creation

Brother sun
With flares of light
Shimmering over miracle mile

Walk softly over this earth
Observe her ways
And give thanks

<u>Maplewood</u>

In the afternoon
I walked a snowy ridge
Overlooking peace chapel
Years and years of shame on my shoulders
Years and years of bridges un-mended

Too much to carry on too far a journey

Leave it here
Says the whisper
At the base of the maple
And follow the birds
Unburdened and unashamed

And so it was
The start of an adventure

To Make Beautiful

Were you not the one?

Drunk on park benches
Howling in the night
Slandering the names of others

Were you not the one?

Lustful for violence
Aroused with hate

Were you not the one?

In strangers arms
While your partner slept
In an empty home

Yes I was

As now I sit
Of sober mind
On driftwood at the shoreline
Waiting calmly
For breath to come

Thus is the justice
Bonaventure spoke of

Trials

Your text books will not help you
Nor all the "isms" you've been taught
And the advice of friends
They cannot tell you
About you

Go out

Where comforts are far from grasp
The fundamentals of life are all that remain
Into the wilderness we travel
To be tried and proved

To observe and consider
To contemplate and imitate
To be still and know

<u>Dolce</u>

Stone Garden
North Shore
Flour and Water
Beechnuts
Testimony
Little Prayers
Monks
Little Flowers
Lucho's Altar
Joe and Dan

Stone Garden

On an old chair beside stone gardens
Light peaks through the trees
A pause in the rhythm tells me
To rest for a short while on my journey
And go in peace

North Shore

We climb up the rock
Standing alone in clouds of blue
Leaping out and laughing
We eat upon the sand
With one another
Wherever two or three
Yet we are all here
The whole earth
Gathered in your name

Flour and Water

In the giving of time
And the giving of resources
Flour and water
Hours we'll never get back
We learn what we didn't know we needed to
To love
The way you have loved

Beechnuts

I let go to rely solely on you
Each day
The way the squirrel under my porch
Arises each morning to meet
My extended hand of beechnuts

Testimony

I rest on rock atop the peak of twin sisters
To fix the plank in my own eye
That I may appropriately respond to the world
Not as a healer
But as testimony of one who has been healed

<u>Little Prayers</u>

With each breath inward
We invite you into this space
To fill the gaps
In conversations and relationships
With your presence
In our hearts
And in our spirit

Monks

The quiet one is like a rare fish
That we spend our lives unknowing if it's there
Yet trying to catch if only one
Who sits still under the banks
Containing all the worlds mystery
We hunt for their presence
That we may come just a bit closer
To you
For a glimpse

Little Flowers

Little flowers on the side of the road
Left there by others
Long ago
Waiting for more little flowers
To be planted by you and I
For a world in need of color

Lucho's Altar

Of hardwood from the surrounding forest
Standing bare and beautiful
In the light of the word
As we ought too
Naked before God
Stripped of all masquerades
Until all that remains
Is Love
Love
Love

Joe and Dan

To walk with you once more
Through fields of grass
To share and listen
As you guide me home

Digestivo

On maple wood pew

He sits before me

Smiling bigger

Than maybe I ever will

Author's Note

I have been incredibly blessed in my life through the power of relationships. I grew up in the woods the way all my friends did, hunting, fishing, and foraging. My friends' impact on my childhood is immeasurable and because of them I have many stories and lessons to share and laugh about. Mentors like Joe and Dan and many others who saw value in me through all of my self-inflicted trials and knew what to say and when to listen. I traveled out west for a while with a fishing pole and a tent and experienced unimaginable joy all because people were willing to show me around and teach me a few things. I've worked in kitchens since then that I never could have imagined being in but there were people there willing to take a chance on me. The outdoors and the world of cooking has given me so much, but it truly is the people who have walked with me that has made everything so special. If there is one piece of advice that I can offer to you it's to muster up the courage to go for it, whatever that is, and be wide eyed and humble through the journey, soak it all in, it's the most worth it thing there is.

I wrote this book for a few reasons. I've wanted to write a book since as far back as I can remember and wrote many things that never quite felt right for me until I began this book. I strongly believe in carrying the torch forward and when Fr. Dan Riley passed away, the idea for this book came to me and I knew that it would be a small part of passing along all that his vision and love gave to me. Finally, I wanted to have something of value to give back to all the people who have made my life so incredibly joyful. To all of those people, I hope you take this as a way of me saying thank you.

> With Love,
> Mike

About The Author

Michael Rickicki is a Catholic by Irish-Italian heritage, cook by trade, and outdoorsman by grace. He lives in Upstate New York.

www.ingramcontent.com/pod-product-compliance
Lightning Source LLC
Chambersburg PA
CBHW060609080526
44585CB00013B/746